The BAD good manners Book

The BAD good manners Book

Babette Cole

PUFFIN BOOKS

Don't leave the taps on in the bathroom.

Don't fill the sink up
with hairs.

Don't bung the loo up with paper.

Don't leave
your toys

on the stairs!

Don't mess around in the kitchen.

Don't dress up the dog ...

or the cat!

Don't have a shampoo

with a big tube of glue,

Do try

to dress
yourself

properly.

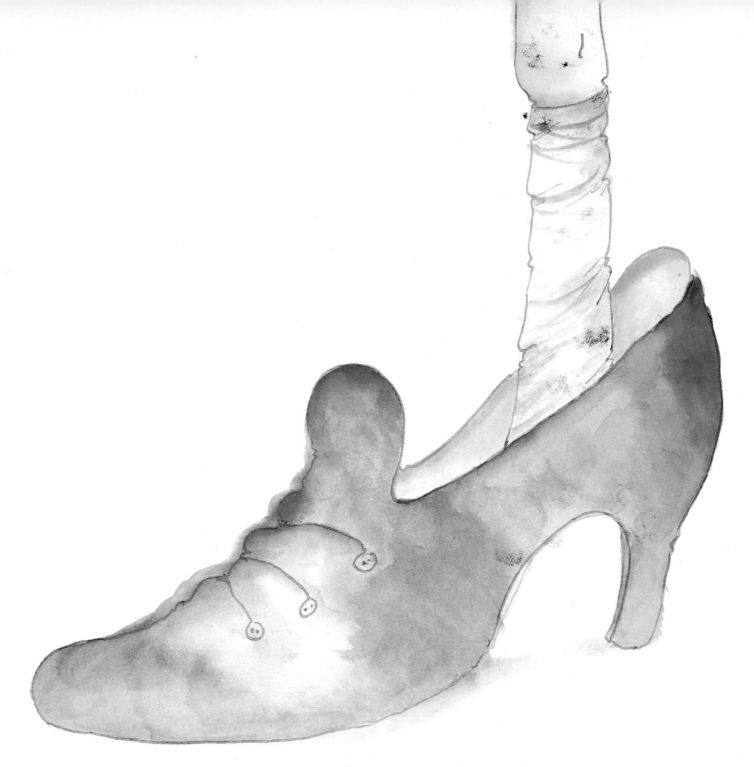

Do put the right shoes

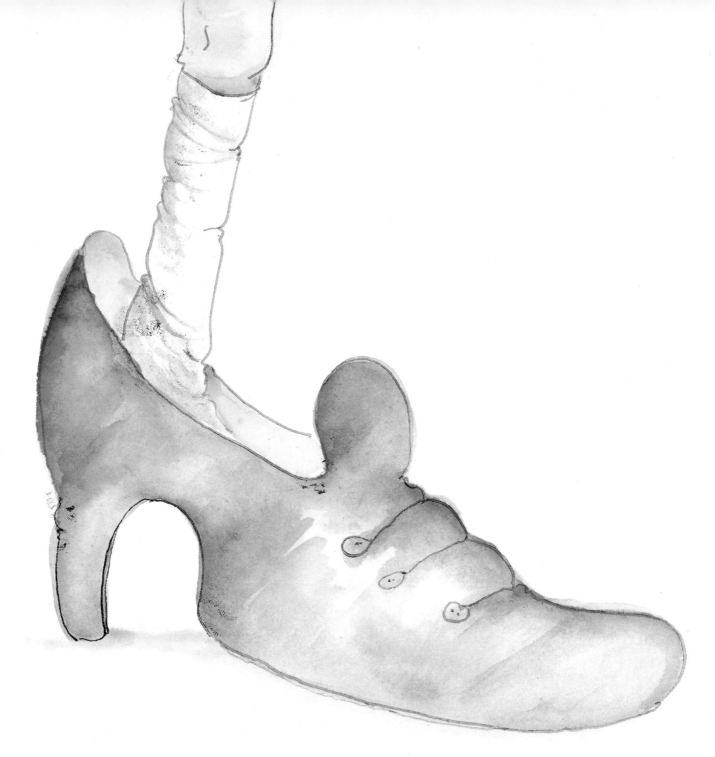

on your feet!

Do try
to mind
your own
business . . .

Do tidy your terrible bedroom.

Brush your hair,

clean
your teeth,

Do as you would
be done by . . .

Z Z Z Z z

BONK!

As much as you possibly can!

"I was trying!"

PUFFIN BOOKS

Published by the Penguin Group
Penguin Books Ltd, 27 Wrights Lane, London W8 5TZ, England
Penguin Putnam Inc., 375 Hudson Street, New York, New York 10014, USA
Penguin Books Australia Ltd, Ringwood, Victoria, Australia
Penguin Books Canada Ltd, 10 Alcorn Avenue, Toronto, Ontario, Canada M4V 3B2
Penguin Books (NZ) Ltd, Private Bag 102902, NSMC, Auckland, New Zealand

Penguin Books Ltd, Registered Offices: Harmondsworth, Middlesex, England

First published by Hamish Hamilton Ltd 1995
Published in Puffin Books 1997
5 7 9 10 8 6

Copyright © Babette Cole, 1995
All rights reserved

The moral right of the author/illustrator has been asserted

Made and printed in Italy by Printer Trento srl